*Sybilla's* MASTODON

# My Mastodon

Barbara Lowell

*illustrated by* Antonio Marinoni

Creative Editions

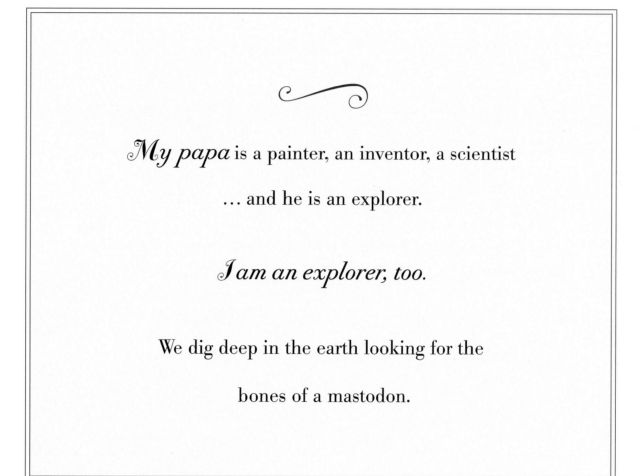

*My papa* is a painter, an inventor, a scientist

… and he is an explorer.

*I am an explorer, too.*

We dig deep in the earth looking for the

bones of a mastodon.

My big brother *Rembrandt* helps. But not as much as I do.

He's too busy bossing me.

"Pay attention, *Sybilla*, you're making a mess," he says.

"It's a messy job, Rembrandt. *No mess, no mastodon.*"

I have a question. But Rembrandt isn't listening, so I ask Papa,

"*What is a mastodon?*"

He says it was an animal like an elephant, but with shaggy hair and

long curving tusks.

It lived so long ago that only its bones are left.

We find lots of those *bones*.

We pile them up in our house.

Mama is fine with that

because …

Our house is a *museum!*

I live with *birds*, *fish*, and other *animals*

from all over the world.

They are very well behaved. They're stuffed.

We explore *jungles* together,

fly high over *mountains*,

and swim the *oceans* in search of treasure.

But then, visitors interrupt our adventures.

They try to pet the animals.

I make a sign.

*We Peales* have important work to do.

We wire the mastodon bones together.

Rembrandt says, "Sybilla, watch what you're doing."

*Some bones are missing.*

We create new ones from wood.

We complete its head with papier-mâché.

When we are done, we step back and take a look.

Our mastodon is *magnificent!*

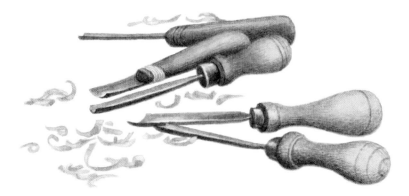

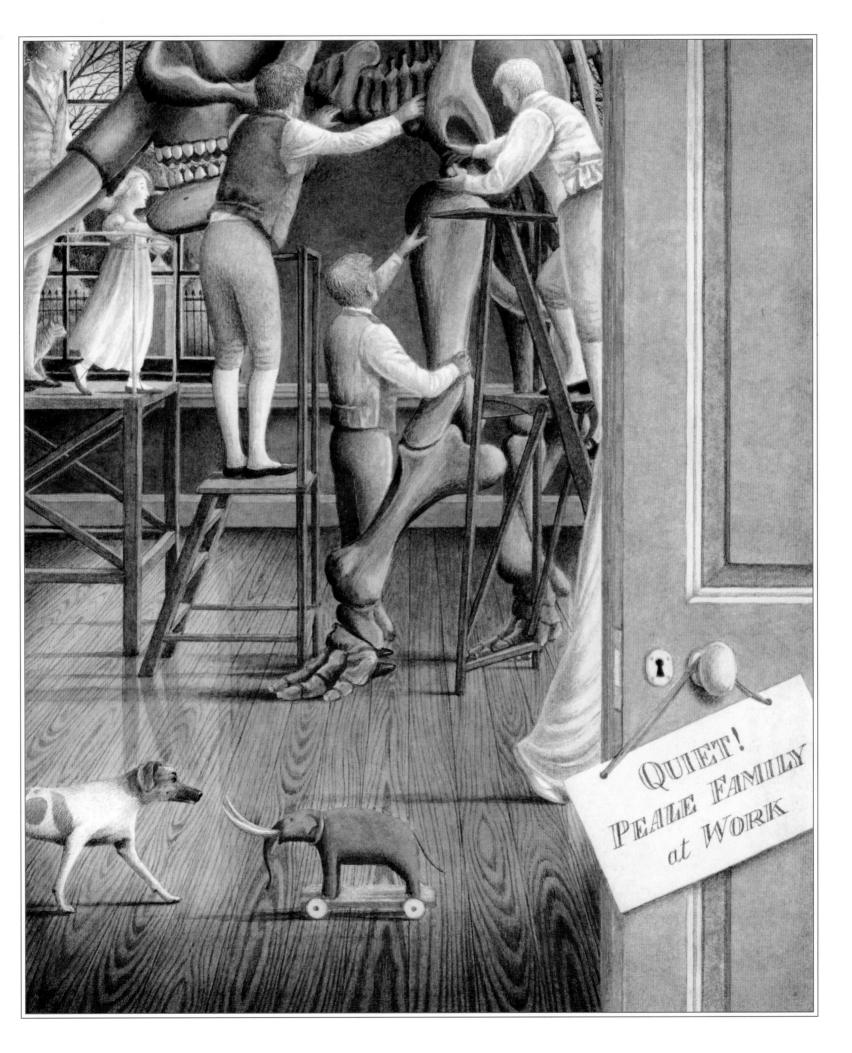

QUIET!
PEALE FAMILY
at WORK

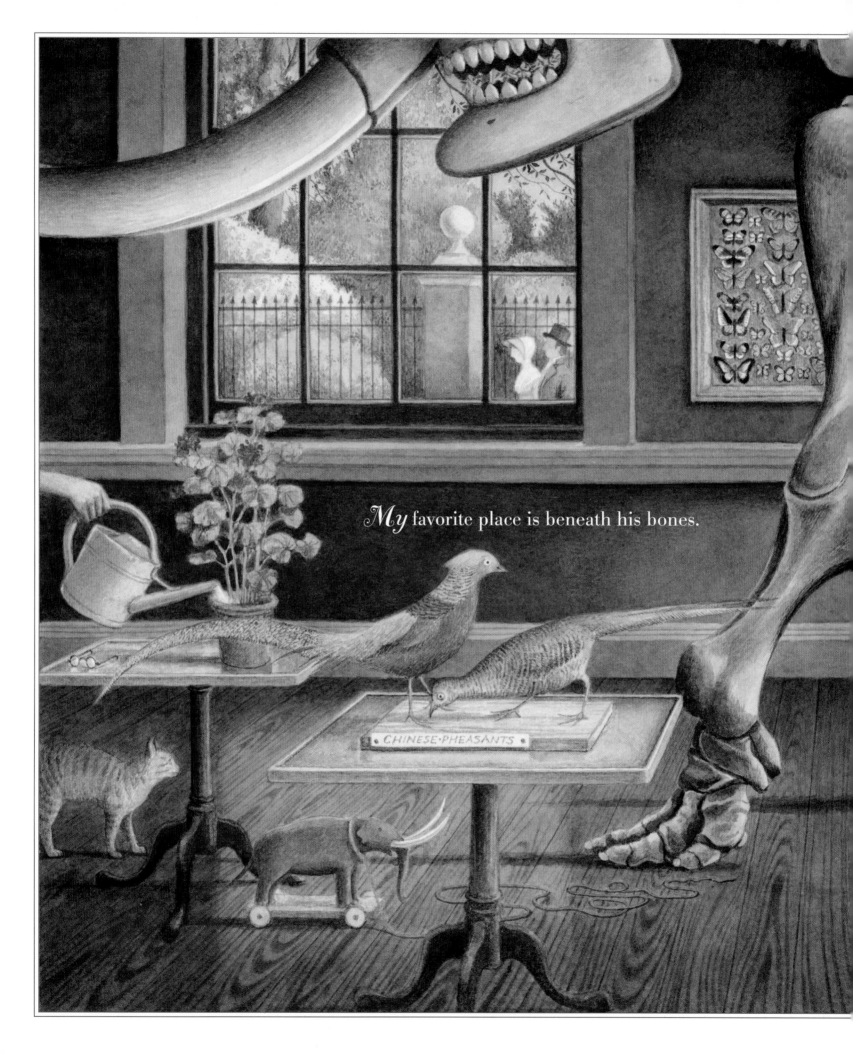

*My* favorite place is beneath his bones.

CHINESE·PHEASANTS

But then, something terrible happens.

My mastodon is invited to London.

Far away. Across the ocean.

Rembrandt wants to take him. Papa agrees.

My mastodon belongs with me.

*He will be lonely.*

And I will miss him. I say no.

But no one listens.

*Rembrandt* works on an advertisement.

"Great American Mastodon to Visit London"

That gives me an idea.

I make my own advertisement.

SYBILLA'S MASTODON
to STAY in PHILADELPHIA

I toss them out the window.

Now everyone will know the good news.

"Clean that mess up," Rembrandt says.

*Fine.* I'll give Rembrandt something else to take to London.

I dip my paintbrush in Papa's brightest red paint.

I make broad strokes and tiny dabs, the way Papa does.

There! A portrait Londoners will line up to see.

I call it: *My Mastodon.*

Rembrandt laughs at me. "They want to see the actual mastodon.

Not a painting."

I curl up beneath my mastodon.

Rembrandt sits down beside me.

"Go away," I tell him.

*He lights a candle.*

"Look, Sybilla."

I peek. My mastodon's shadow flickers on the wall. He's moving!

It is wonderful. But I don't say a word.

"Sybilla, this is for you."

Rembrandt has made a sketch.

"A picture is not the same as having him here," I say.

"It's not real, Sybilla. Anymore."

"He is to me."

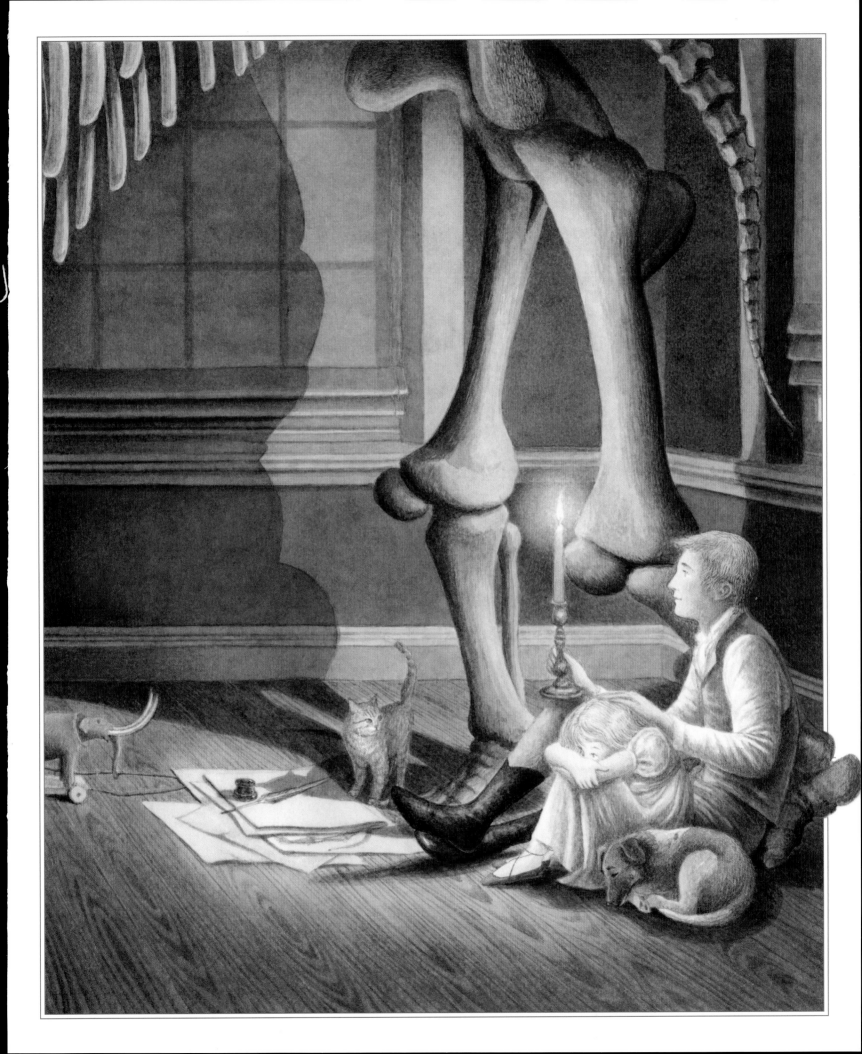

Later, I hear Rembrandt talking to Papa and Mama.

He won't take my mastodon to London.

Because of me.

"I'm disappointed," he tells them.

*My mastodon will stay!*

I'm waiting for a happy feeling inside me.

It doesn't happen.

I don't want Rembrandt to be disappointed.

Even if he is bossy, he is my brother.

*I slip beneath my mastodon.*

And I ask him.

"Would you like to go?

It isn't every day a mastodon visits London.

And makes new friends.

Rembrandt is my brother. He will take good care of you.

And then soon, you will be back home with me."

My mastodon says yes, in his own quiet way.


I know what to do.

I make a new sign.

SYBILLA'S MASTODON
to VISIT LONDON
for a LITTLE WHILE

I show Rembrandt.

He twirls me around.

"This calls for a celebration,"

he says.

*We Peales* know how to celebrate!

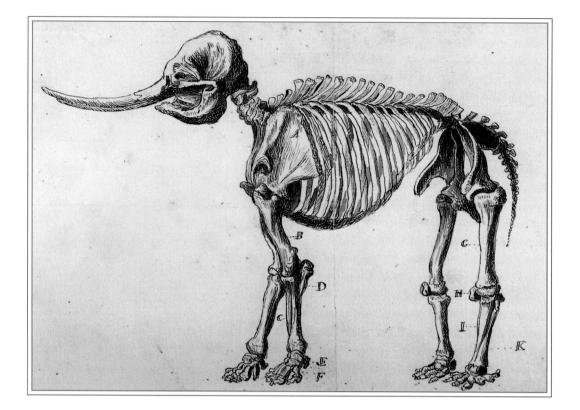

# *Author's Note*

*My Mastodon* is a fictional story inspired by a unique American family, the Peales of Philadelphia.

Sybilla Miriam Peale lived in the Philadelphia Museum—the first natural history museum in America. Unlike European museums at the time, it was open to everyone. Sybilla lived with her family in a separate area of the building but was free to explore every exhibit. She was four years old in 1801, when her father Charles Willson Peale—a well-known artist, naturalist, and museum curator—and her brother Rembrandt led an expedition in New York state to unearth the bones and tusks of the American mastodon. This was the first carefully arranged scientific expedition in America. The Peales uncovered the skeletons of two mastodons (then known as "mammoths").

The bones and tusks were transported to the museum. The skeletons were assembled

and mounted, becoming only the second and third such of their kind displayed in the world. Mr. Peale reported that the larger skeleton was eleven feet tall, fifteen feet long, with ten-foot-long tusks. It weighed more than 1,000 pounds.

Around Christmas of 1801, Mr. Peale opened his mastodon exhibit to the public. Rembrandt and his brother Rubens took the smaller mastodon on a tour of Europe in 1802. Before they left, they celebrated with a dinner under the mastodon's bones.

Mr. Peale's painting, *Exhuming the First American Mastodon*, features members of the Peale family on the right-hand side, holding a drawing of a mastodon bone, with Charles himself gesturing to the site. Rembrandt and Sybilla stand in the middle. The little girl next to Sybilla is her sister Elizabeth (born after the excavation). Rubens is in the top hat behind her, and their oldest brother, Raphaelle, is on the end.

Text copyright © 2020 by Barbara Lowell

Illustrations copyright © 2020 by Antonio Marinoni

Edited by Amy Novesky; designed by Rita Marshall

Photograph on p. 30 from Alamy (FineArt).

Image on p. 31 by Charles Willson Peale, courtesy of the

Maryland Historical Society (Item ID MA5911).

Published in 2020 by Creative Editions

P.O. Box 227, Mankato, MN 56002 USA

Creative Editions is an imprint of The Creative Company

www.thecreativecompany.us

Printed in China

Library of Congress Cataloging-in-Publication Data

Names: Lowell, Barbara, author. / Marinoni, Antonio, illustrator.

Title: My mastodon / by Barbara Lowell; illustrated by Antonio Marinoni.

Summary: Inspired by the 19th-century lives of artist and scientist Charles Willson Peale's

family, this is a tale of a girl and her favorite companion—a fossilized mastodon!

Identifiers: LCCN 2019029593 / ISBN 978-1-56846-327-8

Subjects: CYAC: Family life—Fiction. / Museums—Fiction. / Fossils—Fiction. /

Mastodons—Fiction. / Peale, Charles Willson, 1741–1827—Fiction.

Classification: LCC PZ7.1.L7386 My 2020 / DDC [E]—dc23

First edition 9 8 7 6 5 4 3 2 1